Taking Flight

AF484412

Tilby Susan Thomas

BookLeaf Publishing

India | USA | UK

Taking Flight © 2024 Tilby Susan Thomas

All rights reserved.

No part of this publication may be reproduced, stored in a retrieval system, or transmitted, in any form or by any means, electronic, mechanical, photocopying, recording or otherwise, without the prior written permission of the presenters.

Tilby Susan Thomas asserts the moral right to be identified as author of this work.

Presentation by *BookLeaf Publishing*

Web: www.bookleafpub.com

E-mail: info@bookleafpub.com

ISBN: 9789363318274

First edition 2024

To Amma & Appa, who've made me who I am,

To my sister who's a part of who I am,

To my friends who've accepted me the way I am,

And to those special few coz of whom I am!

ACKNOWLEDGEMENT

First and foremost, I wish to thank my parents for always supporting and encouraging my love for books and reading. Their unwavering belief in me has been a cornerstone in my journey. I know you'll never let me live it down if I don't thank you - so thank you to my annoying but loving sister Tinby for all the madness you add to my life!

My deepest gratitude goes to my teachers over the years, especially my high school principal, Sister Ann Palatty, who inspired my love for the language, and my high school English teacher, Mrs. Swapna Kadam, who showed me the magic hidden in words. I am profoundly grateful to Prof. Rakhee Nair, whose guidance helped sustain my passion for words even during my engineering years. A special mention goes to two of my engineering professors, Prof. Onkar Sahasrabudhe and Dr. Sandeep Joshi, who reaffirmed my confidence to pursue my dreams.

To my friends who have not just tolerated, but also embraced my idiosyncrasies, I love you guys. Thank you Rajeev for being the voice in my head and my safe space. Abhijit & Paresh - I treasure our endless conversations about everything under the sun, from trees to the seas. Aakash, Alankrita & Jenny, thank you for always believing in me, even when I doubt myself. Zaki & Parth, your promise to be the first to ensure I have a best-seller means the world to me (and I will hold you to it, even if you were kidding). I also want to extend my thanks to a few special individuals who became unexpected friends and brought joy to my days - Priyanka & Bhakti. Your presence has been a delightful surprise! Sydelle, Isha, Rochelle, Moriska & Danielle, thank you girls for being among my first cheerleaders and boosting my confidence.

Lastly, but certainly not least, I am deeply grateful to BookLeaf Publishing for their #TheWriteAngle challenge. This initiative finally pushed me to work towards my dream of publishing this book.

Thank you all for being part of my journey.

PREFACE

Every poem in this collection is a labour of love and every line is an attempt to express a heartfelt emotion. Love and its pain, joy and grief, hope and fear, even gratitude and anger, have all found their way into the words on these pages.

This is a collection of random musings that I've tried to express as words on a page. These poems are a reflection of what I think, how I feel and who I am...they open a tiny window to give a glimpse into my soul...

I believe words hold immense power and beauty that can both create and destroy the world. I hope my poems speak to you and find a home in your hearts!

"Once you have tasted flight, you will forever walk the earth with your eyes turned skyward, for there you have been, and there you will always long to return."
– Leonardo da Vinci

Wake-up Call

Painted red, this mouth can do more than just
kiss,
It forms words you shouldn't miss!
You can't stop them from spilling out,
It can't be silenced, you can't ignore the shout!

Stop the ignorant - the ones spreading hate,
Stop them before it's too late!
Stop those trying to break us down,
Those trying to separate us from our own!

Open your eyes, rip out the blindfold,
Don't blindly believe everything you are told!
Realize we are one, it's love we must uphold,
Wake up before 'The Powers That Be' condone
actions that stop our heart cold!

Truth

Knowing you has changed me, changed who I
am.
I don't want to own you,
Nor do I need to make you mine!
I know my heart belongs to you,
I know who I am because of you...

My love needs no validation
It needs no proof
It does not demand reciprocation
My love is complete as it is!

The burden I wore has finally lifted,
I can give voice to my truth,
I never wish to cause you despair,
Know that I'll always be there...

I've fought heaven and hell to keep you safe
I've fallen from grace!
I've been broken and punished,
I'd do it all over again!

Happiness isn't in the having,
It's in the being,
It's in just saying it.

My truth has set me free,
This is for the world to know -
I LOVE YOU!!!
And my happiness has been in loving you...

My Heart Belongs To The Sky

I am blue...
And my love is true;
It is not a force you can subdue!

My love is infinite, it is limitless;
Like the sea - deep and endless,
Like the sky - vast and boundless!

To be by your side - is all I long;
The sound of your name is my heart's song;
Only to you does my love belong!

My soul knows no limits, it wants to fly;
To no rule does it want to comply;
For the truth is simple - my heart belongs to the
sky!!

I Love You

5

Normalize saying "I love you"
To friends, your family, your partner,
and all those you love.
Say it not to hear it back,
Say it not as a question
awaiting its answer.
Say it because it's your truth,
Say it because it's yours alone.
Say it out loud,
Say it out proud!
Say it to soothe
the ache in your heart,
Say it to celebrate
the joy in your soul.
Say "I love you"
because you mean it.
Say "I love you"
because they need to hear it.
Say "I love you"
because these are the words that
hold the very foundation of the universe...

Holding On

Ghosts of moments past,
Whispering constantly in my ear.
Laughing, jeering, taunting, haunting...

Dangling the past to relive the pure joy,
A chance to touch personified temptation.
Laughing, jeering, taunting, haunting...

Time, that fickle mistress, she's laughing,
Reminding me of passing years, haunting...
I cling on to the fleeting moments with fingers
trembling,
Because to lose them would mean I'm truly
dying...

A sudden urge to taste the memory,
The stabbing pain of an unbidden epiphany.
Trembling, shattering, hurting, dying...

The heart-wrenching pain of the unknown,
Struggling to breathe on, unwilling to let go.
Yes, I'm trembling, shattering, hurting, dying...

Don't - DO NOT

Hey Baby Girl,
DO NOT let the safety of an embrace
be marred by a forceful grasp.
DO NOT let the pleasure of sweet caresses
be tarnished by groping hands.
DO NOT let the joy of a gentle touch
be ruined by bruising fingers.
DO NOT let the memory of loving hands
be overshadowed by an unwanted grip.
DO NOT let the hope of a happy tomorrow
be snatched by a cruel present.

Hey Baby Girl,
DO NOT blame yourself for the actions of
others,
nor for their reactions.
DO NOT blame yourself for their words,
nor for their judgements.
DO NOT blame yourself for their silence,
nor for their indifference.
DO NOT blame yourself for their insincerity,
nor for their ignorance.

Hey Baby Girl,
DO NOT let the world dim your dreams,

DO NOT let the world silence your words,
DO NOT let the world steal your thunder,
DO NOT let the world crush your hope!!

I am THEM

9

The rage of the women long forgotten,
Mixed with the soil, runs through my veins.
The voices of the women cruelly silenced,
Find their home in the echoes of my words.
The dreams of the women thoughtlessly crushed,
Find their wings in the sparkle in my eyes.
The spirits of the women who dared to defy,
Find their abode in the strength of my will.
The stories of the women carelessly erased,
Find their destiny fulfilled in the life I dare to
build.

Fly High

Return to dust I must someday...
So why not soar the sky today?
Fear grips my heart, I may never really fly,
But damned will I be if I never try!
A spark of life in a single moment;
To spare me the regret, the lifelong torment.
Feel the breathless head rush, the hammering
heartbeat,
Assure myself I did not live my entire life in the
back seat.
Taste joy, for even a brief while, the urge
impossible to resist...
Be alive, if just for a moment, than be doomed
to merely exist!

Angel

They say I am an angel, a wavelength of
celestial intent
They say I was a good soldier
They say I pulled you out of hell
They say I was lost when I first laid hands on
you...

You say I am your best friend
You say I healed your wounds
You say I make you smile
You say I saved you...

I say I am whoever you want me to be
I say I always come when you call
I say I'll go with you to the end of the world
I say I am and will always be yours!

Only LOVE Can Save Us

We are a generation of reluctant adults,
Waiting for an opportunity to throw away
The blanket of obligations and expectations,
To spread our wings and seize the sky...

We are a generation of reluctant adults,
Waiting to make sure that no one snatches away
Our freedom to dream,
Clip our wings before we rise and fly...

We are a generation of reluctant adults,
Waiting for someone to really see us
And love the child in us,
Because we know - Only LOVE can save us!

The Storm

Looking at the gathering storm;
Dark clouds, crashing thunder,
Flashes lighting up the sky,
The downpour stinging bare skin...

She looked up
And let it wash over her,
The thunder resonating with each heartbeat
Every strike of lightning bringing a new
memory...

She wondered
Which could cause more destruction -
The storm around her
Or the one raging in her heart...??

Not in Vain

Each heartbeat is a story in itself,
Every breath a lifetime...
You never know how long you have,
So treasure each moment while it lasts...

It's not a give and take,
It's not about what you can gain...
The magic is in knowing
You gave your all and kept going...

Life might disappear in just a blink,
Do not give a chance for regret...
There's nothing to lose,
So go ahead and say it!

Three simple words may give hope to a soul,
Let them know they are not alone...
And if you don't get it back, just know,
You didn't live in vain, but loved a soul!
And when you go, that's all that'll remain -
A love, a breath, a heartbeat no more....

Wish

15

I do not want a love that lasts forever,
Just moments that'll be forgotten never.
I know not what the future holds in store,
The ocean is vast and I'm at the shore...

I do not need a promise of eternity,
Just someone who can love with integrity.
Give me just a few happy moments together,
And I promise they'll be a part of me forever...

I do not ask for much,
Simply to understand me as such.
Someone who knows my every heartbeat,
I'll place the world at his feet!

Forever

Sometimes forever is wrapped
Inside small moments,
Sometimes lasting
Just a few heartbeats...

But they are enough
To quench
The longing
In your soul...

And you can survive
A lifetime
With just the memory
Of forever...

Fairytale

17

Forever is just a fairytale,
A myth meant to regale...
What matters is only this moment,
Accept this truth to avoid torment...
Life cannot be lived tomorrow,
So enjoy today - both joy and sorrow...

Alliteration

18

Sometimes,
Even everything
is not
Enough.

Silence

Silence is -
The cruelest punishment
The harshest criticism
The loudest scream
The final goodbye...

What Do You Do?

What do you do -
When hope loses hope?
When trust breaks trust?
When faith destroys faith?

What do you do -
When kindness revokes kindness?
When acceptance belittles acceptance?
When understanding stops understanding?

What do you do -
When love hurts love?
When love outlives love?
When love outgrows love?

How do you go on
When you aren't you anymore...??

Hidden

21

Unshed tears stinging my eyes...
Unsaid words clogging up my throat...
Unasked questions scalding my tongue...
Unspoken confessions threatening to spill from
my lips...
Unnoticed me waiting for someone to peel away
the layers...
Unveil the girl hidden for so long in the
encompassing shadows...

LOVE

They say the greatest gift of all is love,
Given to us from the One above...
They say love is all powerful,
The feeling oh so wonderful...

But I know love is not all smiles and roses,
A threat so real and huge it poses...
Love can truly shatter your heart,
Force you to wrap pain as art!

They say true love is a boon,
None to its charm are yet immune...
They say true love is rare,
Not many can their heart truly share...

I know love is not just a noun,
Not just a fancy flower crown...
It is a verb that demands action,
Needs both words and gestures, in repetition...

They say love conquers all,
I know love can lead to a fall...
They say love makes everything alright,
I know love is my leading light...

Yes love is scary and love is hard,
Love is not just a pretty word on a card!
Love is true and love is right,
It adds beauty to life infinite...
Everything you do, do it for love,
And you'll find that - to live is to love!

Alive or A Lie?

Who knows what's true?
What is the hidden lie?
Can you believe life isn't tricky
When it's testing you every day?

Surrounded by words,
Yet drowning in the silence...
The cost of survival - too high,
When everything you know
Seems to disappear...
When what you believed to be real
Turns out to be just a mirage...
How can you be sure you are alive
And not merely existing??

www.ingramcontent.com/pod-product-compliance
Lightning Source LLC
Chambersburg PA
CBHW071240140726
47996CB00007B/2687